JAZZ MASTERS

Sonny Rollins

by Charley Gerard

Consolidated Music Publishers

New York • London • Tokyo • Sydney • Cologne

Cover design by Barbara Hoffman
Cover photography by David Gahr

e d c b a

International Standard Book Number: 0-8256-4200-0

Distributed throughout the world by Music Sales Corporation:

33 West 60th Street, New York 10023
78 Newman Street, London W1P 3LA
4-26-22 Jingumae, Shibuya-ku, Tokyo 150
27 Clarendon Street, Artarmon, Sydney NSW 2064
Kölner Strasse 199, D-5000 Cologne 90

Contents

A Note on the Transcriptions

In this edition all of the solos are transposed for B♭ tenor saxophone. The chord symbols are given in the transposed key to relate to the melody line as written. A separate edition (Music for Millions Series 86/040086) is available, containing the same material transcribed for all C (nontransposing) instruments.

Sonny Rollins

For three decades the music of Sonny Rollins has impressed audiences, including many jazz greats. He is a legendary figure who has twice disappeared from the jazz scene. Rollins has put his personal stamp on ballads, blues, bebop, calypso, modal jazz, free jazz, and jazz-rock. He is a virtuoso tenor saxophonist, composer, and the leading exponent of thematic improvisation.

Sonny Rollins was born on September 9, 1929 in NYC. In 1944, while studying music in high school, he took up the alto sax, switching to tenor two years later. While still in his teens he started working professionally in the New York area. He stayed with the tenor sax, although he can be heard on alto and soprano on some of his recent recordings. His first recording was with singer Babs Gonzales in 1948, and soon after, he recorded with pianist Bud Powell, trumpeter Fats Navarro, and trombonist J.J. Johnson—all highly influential bebop players. After working with drummer Art Blakey, pianist/ arranger Tadd Dameron, and trumpeter Miles Davis (with whom he recorded some records which are now collectors' items), he began his famous collaboration with drummer Max Roach in 1956. Subsequently Rollins formed his own group, using Max Roach as a featured sideman on many of his recordings. In the mid-fifties he also performed and recorded with pianist/composer Thelonious Monk.

As with most saxophonists who began playing in the bebop era, Rollins's first recordings are reminiscent of Charlie Parker. By 1956, possibly by a natural maturation process or because Rollins had had the opportunity to play with the most influential jazz musicians of his time, his music took on the distinctive sound for which it is now famous. At this time he recorded *Jazz Colossus*, one of the all-time great jazz albums. After the release of this record his reputation began to grow internationally. In 1959, at the height of acclaim, he dropped out of the jazz scene. During this period a few passersby had the luck to hear him practicing early in the morning on the Williamsburg Bridge in NYC.

Rollins emerged from obscurity two years later with *The Bridge*, an album which turned a generation of tenor players around. On this album Rollins concentrates on the difficult lower tones of the sax, adding a whole new dimension to his playing. Up to the time of this recording, the beauty of the lower register had been greatly ignored. Although revolutionary in this respect, the album basically held to the hard bop tradition of the late fifties. For this reason his first public appearance on returning to the scene was a surprise. Rollins fronted a group of Ornette Coleman sidemen including trumpeter Don Cherry and played free form. This began a series of avant-garde performances followed by his second disappearance from public life.

Rollins's tenacious creativity was bound to resurface again and as the jazz scene changed it did just that, but in a new form. On returning, he recorded *Next Album* on which he used electric instruments for the first time. Since then, his performances have demonstrated his ability to bring a distinctive sound to many types of jazz. His playing is no longer confined to any one tradition. Rollins has not only survived three decades and several eras of jazz, but he has played an important role in all of them.

I hope you enjoy reading this book as much as I enjoyed writing it. I couldn't have done it without the invaluable aid of my wife, Judith Weinstock.

CHARLEY GERARD
Tampico, Tamaulipas
Mexico
May 1979

Notes on the Solos

You Don't Know What Love Is (1956)

With Tommy Flanagan, piano; Doug Watkins, bass; Max Roach, drums. This is a good example of Rollins's ballad style. Parts of the second and third choruses are in double time.

Transcription in this book: complete first solo.

Alfie's Theme (1966)

With a big band arrangement by Oliver Nelson, including solos by pianist Roger Kellaway and guitarist Kenny Burrell. The music was written for the film *Alfie*. It contains one of Sonny Rollins's most famous solos, large excerpts of which appear in this book.

On Impulse (1966)

Same personnel as above. Rollins is featured here in a fast jazz waltz. The piece concludes with a cadenza against held chords, which comes to a surprisingly abrupt end.

Transcription: complete solo.

Blessing in Disguise (1966)

With Jimmy Garrison, bass; Elvin Jones, drums. The pianoless group is a favorite of Rollins. This piece is an excellent example of thematic improvisation, and I have transcribed several sections of the solo to show how it develops.

East Broadway Run Down (1966)

Same personnel as above with Freddie Hubbard, trumpet. This is one of Rollins's most avant-garde performances. It gives the feeling of a run-down part of lower Manhattan. After a strange tune arranged for trumpet and tenor saxophone mostly in fourths, the piece starts out as a blues and then becomes totally free. Every time the listener thinks it's going to end, Rollins starts up again. In parts of this long piece, Rollins plays only on the mouthpiece.

Transcription: five blues choruses.

The Everywhere Calypso (1972)

With George Cables, piano; Bob Cranshaw, bass; David Lee, drums; Arthur Jenkins, conga drums and percussion. This is one of many calypso tunes recorded by Rollins, whose heritage is West Indian. The most famous one is Rollins's "St. Thomas."

Transcription: complete first solo.

Playin' in the Yard (1972)

Same personnel as above, with drummer Jack de Johnette replacing David Lee. Rollins is in a funky rock mood here.

Transcription: complete first solo.

Keep Hold of Yourself (1962)

Same personnel as above without Arthur Jenkins. This is a minor modal blues.

Transcription: four choruses.

God Bless the Child (1962)

With Jim Hall, guitar, and others. See the transcription for more information.

Symbols and Terms

  Lip slurs or glides going up to or down from a note. Rollins uses these a lot.

gliss. *Glissando*: a rapidly played chromatic scale.

  Clipped attack: one of the main ingredients of Rollins's individualistic style.

vib. *Vibrato.*

Chord Symbols

Ma, no symbol used: major
m, —: minor
aug, +: augmented
°, dim7: diminished seventh
dim, —: diminished interval
Ma7: major seventh
7: dominant seventh
m7, —7: minor seventh
ø7: half-diminished seventh
sus: suspended

You Don't Know What Love Is

Don Raye
Gene de Paul

9

3rd chorus

piano solo

Alfie's Theme

Sonny Rollins

*Use low B♭ fingering.

(accompanied by
piano, bass, drum)

15

On Impulse

Sonny Rollins

Blessing in Disguise

Sonny Rollins

27

East Broadway Run Down

Sonny Rollins

*Trumpet actually sounds a ninth lower than written.

The Everywhere Calypso

Sonny Rollins

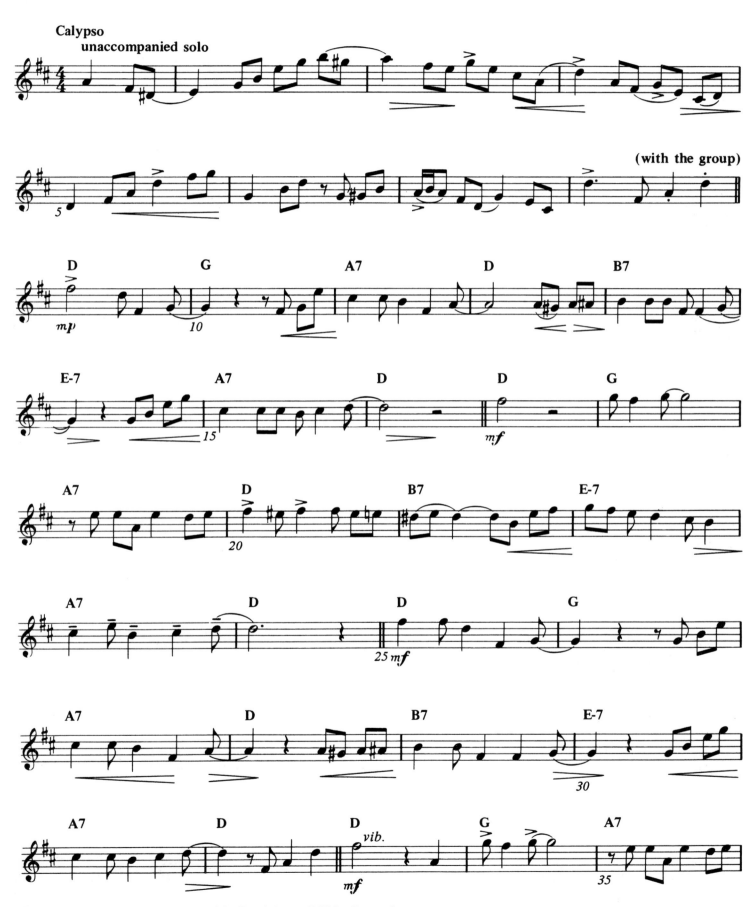

34

Playin' in the Yard

Sonny Rollins

Keep Hold of Yourself

Sonny Rollins

An Analysis of Sonny Rollins's Style

As with all great jazz musicians, Sonny Rollins's sound is instantly recognizable. The main features of his music are cello-like tone with little vibrato, rhythmic complexity, harmonic sophistication, sarcastic wit, and an overriding sense of form. Many of his compositions—"St. Thomas," "Doxy," and "Alfie's Theme" come to mind—are singable melodies with simple harmonies which allow him the freedom to improvise variations. It's very common for Rollins to repeat the melody verbatim or in an altered but recognizable form. In his solos he also plays melodies evocative of the twenties and thirties, sometimes quoting old tunes.

Rollins takes several approaches to chord changes: chordal, scalar, playing out of the changes, or a combination of these. The approach he takes has a lot to do with the chord changes or mood of the tune. For example, the solo on "The Everywhere Calypso" is almost entirely a chordal improvisation, which Rollins might have chosen in order to suggest a traditional West Indian feeling. On the other hand. Rollins's solo on "Alfie's Theme" contains large-out-of-the-changes passages. Playing out of the changes almost automatically gives a solo an avant-garde quality since it rejects the harmonic limitations of the chord changes. Another factor is the instrumentation of the group. In general, a soloist working in front of a pianist, big band, or (to a lesser extent) guitar, has less harmonic freedom than one working without this chordal background. For this reason, Rollins's earlier recordings, made with just bass and drums, provided him with a setting in which he could explore certain ideas freely.

The endings of Sonny Rollins's pieces are very unpredictable. Just when one thinks he's stopped, he starts up again, providing an anticlimax. The pieces either trail off, leaving us with the feeling that the music could continue forever, or terminate without warning. Although Rollins's propensity for anticlimax might be attributed to a sarcastic nature, he also has the ability to be highly romantic, as can be heard in the ballads he has recorded, such as "You Don't Know What Love Is," " 'Til There Was You," and many others. He is an inventive player and is just as creative at lightning fast speeds as at slow tempos. In fact, he is so versatile a musician that he is as comfortable with avant-garde music as he is with something more standard. But no matter what he plays, he always sounds like Sonny Rollins—fabulous!

Chordal Improvisation: Arpeggios

In a totally chordal improvisation each note is part of the chord which is indicated. In other words, where there is a Dm7, the main notes are D, F, A, and C, and all non-chord notes must resolve to them. The most basic way of playing chord changes is restricting oneself to the chord tones alone. Sonny Rollins frequently takes this approach. The following are the kinds of arpeggios (broken chords) which Rollins plays:

1. Arpeggios containing only simple chord tones.
2. Arpeggios containing tones from more complex (higher-number) chords.
3. Arpeggios containing non-chord tones which clash with the indicated chord.

In this section I have listed major, major seventh, minor, and minor seventh arpeggios, minor arpeggios with ninth added, dominant seventh, dominant ninth, and diminished seventh arpeggios, and several miscellaneous ones. Where no explanation appears, the arpeggios contain only chord tones.

Major

This F major arpeggio clashes with both Fm7 and Bb 7.

"On Impulse"

"Blessing in Disguise"

"East Broadway Run Down"

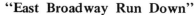

The Db major arpeggio clashes with Gb 7 in the fifth measure.

"East Broadway Run Down"

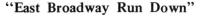

"The Everywhere Calypso"

"The Everywhere Calypso"

The D arpeggio extends an eighth note into the G measure.

"The Everywhere Calypso"

Major Seventh

An Em7 arpeggio is followed by a CMa7 arpeggio.

"You Don't Know What Love Is"

An A♭Ma7 arpeggio is used with B♭7 to form B♭13.

"On Impulse"

A GMa7 arpeggio is used with Em7 to form Em9.

"On Impulse"

"Blessing in Disguise"

Minor

An F♯ minor arpeggio is followed by an E minor arpeggio, both being chords that naturally occur in the key of D.

"On Impulse"

A G♯ minor arpeggio combines with B to form B6.

"Blessing in Disguise"

"The Everywhere Calypso"

"The Everywhere Calypso"

"The Everywhere Calypso"

Minor Seventh

This A♭ m7 arpeggio is the minor seventh substitution for D♭ 7.

"You Don't Know What Love Is"

An Fm7 arpeggio is used with D, then with Em7. It forms a DMa9 with the D chord, and an Em13 with the Em7.

"On Impulse"

A Bm7 arpeggio combines with Em7 to form Em11.

"On Impulse"

Minor Arpeggios with the Ninth Added

This D♭ minor arpeggio with the ninth added combines with G♭7 to form G♭7($^{13}_9$).

"You Don't Know What Love Is"

When this E minor arpeggio with the ninth added combines with A7 it forms A7($^{13}_9$).

"On Impulse"

Dominant Seventh

"Blessing in Disguise"

"The Everywhere Calypso"

Dominant Ninth

"The Everywhere Calypso"

Diminished Seventh

A D♯ dim 7 arpeggio combines with B7 to form B7(−9) in the following examples.

"The Everywhere Calypso"

"The Everywhere Calypso"

Miscellaneous

This A♭ m9 (ma7) combines with D♭ 7 to form D♭ 7(+$^{13}_{11}$$_{9}$).

"You Don't Know What Love Is"

This F♭ augmented arpeggio combines with G♭ 7 to form G♭

"You Don't Know What Love Is"

Major, minor, and diminished arpeggios are consecutively used against F minor.

"You Don't Know What Love Is"

An Fm6 with the ninth added used dissonantly on A7.

"Keep Hold of Yourself"

Scalar Improvisation

Since the late fifties jazz musicians have been interested in scalar improvisation. Using this technique Sonny Rollins restricts himself to the notes in a particular scale, and plays them over one or several chords. The scale notes may go nicely with the chords (consonant) or may be very jarring (dissonant). The scales and Rollins's placement of them is worth analyzing. I have added Roman numeral chord symbols to facilitate transposition.

1. Whole-tone scale based on C (V) on C7 (V7) preceding F minor (I minor).

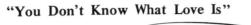

2. Phrygian scale on G (III) with Fm7 (IIm7) to B♭ 7 (V7).

3. Pentatonic scale with occasional blues note—E♭ (♭V)—with A7 (I7) to D7 (IV7).

46

4. Pentatonic scale used with a minor blues.

"Keep Hold of Yourself"

5. Scales containing notes that are dissonant with the chords on which they are played. (Dissonant notes are circled.)

"On Impulse" whole tone scale

"On Impulse" major scale

Sequences

Sonny Rollins, like many other bebop and hard bop saxophonists, often plays a riff and then transposes it. This technique is called sequence.

Type 1: The phrase is transposed with the same rhythms. Of this type there are *real sequences,* those that are unaltered, and *tonal sequences,* those where the intervals are slightly altered to stay within the key.

Type 2: The phrase is transposed as a *real sequence* or a *tonal sequence,* but with different rhythms.

Type 3: The phrase is not transposed note-for-note, although it is very similar to the original and the melodic contour and rhythms are maintained.

"On Impulse"

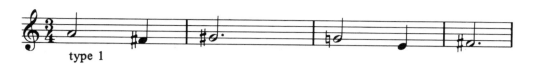

type 1

"East Broadway Run Down"

type 2

"The Everywhere Calypso"

type 1

Playing out of the Changes

In any solo where the harmonic structure is limited, it is possible to leave the chords behind for a while and then return to them. This is called playing out of the changes. Sonny Rollins and John Coltrane are perhaps the two best-known saxophonists who have mastered this technique. When playing out of the changes, Rollins may employ one of the following:

1. Substitute changes a fixed interval from the original
2. Melodic devices such as repetition and sequence
3. Free playing

Example of No. 1. In the excerpt below, Rollins plays substitute changes a diminished fifth higher than the original.

"On Impulse"

Example of No. 2. The following passage consists of a motif which Rollins repeats or alters several times. The passage is not related harmonically to the chords with which it is played.

"Alfie's Theme"

Rollins also uses sequences in his out-of-the-changes sections, as in this excerpt.

"Alfie's Theme"

Example of No. 3. The following three passages are from Rollins's solo on "Alfie's Theme," which is based on one chord, C minor. In these out-of-the-changes passages he leaves C minor for a couple of measures and then returns.

Thematic Improvisation

In this type of improvisation, the theme, not just its harmonies (as in regular jazz improvisations) is used as the basis of the solo. Rollins's solos are logically constructed and integrated rather than being a string of unrelated choruses. The following are the themes from "Alfie's Theme," "Blessing in Disguise," and "Keep Hold of Youself." Each theme is followed by several variations, which demonstrate Rollins's incredible ability to sustain a mood by using slightly altered repetitions of a theme. Thus, Rollins uses a minimum of musical material for a sustained effect. In these next excerpts, the variations on the theme are bracketed.

Most of these variations are based on the last two measures of the tune. The last variation is on the entire theme.

"Alfie's Theme"

This next is an example of a rubato (out-of-tempo) theme. Rollins uses a lot of rhythmic regrouping here: The same tones are used with different rhythmic values. For example, compare the first few notes of the theme and the beginnings of several variations. You'll notice the notes are similar but the rhythms are totally different.

"Blessing in Disguise"

"Blessing in Disguise" is an *"a tempo"* theme. Variation 1 is the same as the original theme but with a slightly longer last note. (Not printed below are differences in articulation in otherwise identical reproductions of the theme.) In variations 2 through 5, new pitches are often substituted, but the melodic contour and rhythmic quality of the original is the same. Variations 6 through 8 are four measures long instead of two, and each successive variation shows more alterations.

"Blessing in Disguise"

*An extension is the occasional lengthening or widening-out of a phrase.

This twelve-measure blues is followed by only one variation in which slight rhythmic and note changes are worth comparing measure by measure.

"Keep Hold of Yourself"

Rhythmic Devices: Syncopation and Delay

Syncopation is a cornerstone of jazz and popular music, and delay—playing behind the beat—is a device you're likely to hear on a lot of jazz albums. Other rhythmic devices like displacement and regrouping can be found in the section on Repetitive Phrases.

In music having a steady basic meter ($\frac{4}{4}$ or $\frac{3}{4}$, for example) syncopation is when a normally unaccented beat (2 and 4 in $\frac{4}{4}$) or a subdivision of the beat (an eighth note or a sixteenth note) is accented.

accent on 2 and 4:

accent on subdivisions of the beat:

Often, syncopated music gives the effect of a series of different meters.

sounds like:

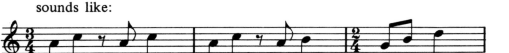

The following are examples of syncopation taken from Sonny Rollins's solos.

"You Don't Know What Love Is"

"Alfie's Theme"

"Alfie's Theme"

"On Impulse"

"Blessing in Disguise"

"Blessing in Disguise"

"East Broadway Run Down"

"East Broadway Run Down"

"The Everywhere Calypso"

"The Everywhere Calypso"

"Keep Hold of Yourself"

"Keep Hold of Yourself"

sounds like:

"Keep Hold of Yourself"

"Delay" is the term I use for playing behind the beat. In ballads, Rollins often drags the tune behind the beat, playing the notes after we expect to hear them. He usually slows down the tune by playing a lot of grace notes and lip slurs, amply demonstrated in the following examples from "You Don't Know What Love Is." I have written the delayed passage first, then rewritten it the way we expect to hear it due to our memory of the tune. We expect the C to fall on G♭ 7 instead of an eighth note later.

We expect the Gs to fall on the first beats of both measures. Both are delayed.

We expect the C to fall on G♭ 7, and the last F to fall on the first beat on D♭7.

We expect the final C to fall on A♭ 6, not later.

We expect the melody to begin with G on the first beat on F minor, instead of on the third beat.

Here we expect the D♭ to fall on the third beat on G♭ 7.

In fast tempos Rollins sometimes slows down his sixteenth notes to form triplets. Since the triplets retain the standard jazz phrasing (I call it "reverse slurring") for sixteenth notes— —they consequently sound like them.

"Blessing in Disguise"

sounds like:

Phrase Repetition

Repetition fixes the listener's attention on a melody and lodges it in his mind. It has always been an important aspect of popular music and jazz. Sonny Rollins uses repetition in the following ways:

Type 1: Real, note-for-note repetition, such as in "Blessing in Disguise."

Type 2: Rollins is an expert juggler of rhythms, and often uses rhythmic displacement to syncopate his music. That is, he repeats a phrase beginning off the beat if the phrase started on the beat, and on the beat if it started off the beat. Many jazz and rock musicians playing in $\frac{4}{4}$ use repeated figures 1½ beats long, beginning on different parts of the beat with each repetition.

This gives a polyrhythmic feeling suggesting triple time, although the meter is $\frac{4}{4}$.

Type 3: Repetition of one note.

Type 4: Alternation between two notes.

Type 5: Rhythmic regrouping. The tones, but not the rhythms, are maintained in the repetition.

"You Don't Know What Love Is"

"Alfie's Theme"

"On Impulse"

"Blessing in Disguise"

61

"East Broadway Run Down"

"The Everywhere Calypso"

"Playin' in the Yard"

Anticipation

Anticipation (ANT) is the sounding of a note or notes before the chord to which it belongs. This device is most common in dominant to tonic (V to I) or subdominant to tonic (IV to I) progressions. The anticipating notes usually occur directly before the anticipated chord.

"On Impulse"

"Blessing in Disguise"

"Blessing in Disguise"

"Blessing in Disguise"

"East Broadway Run Down"

"East Broadway Run Down"

"The Everywhere Calypso"

"The Everywhere Calypso"

"Playin' in the Yard"

The following are three anticipations which occur in progressions other than dominant or subdominant to tonic, and are more dissonant than anticipations which occur there.

"On Impulse"

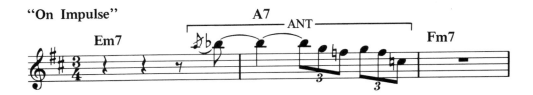

"East Broadway Run Down"

"The Everywhere Calypso"

Delayed Resolution

Sometimes Rollins continues to play in a harmony after it has changed (DR). The C in the second measure belongs with B♭7. Although it is not a chord member of B♭7 it is a common added tone to B♭7 forming B♭9. It resolves down to B, the fifth of Em7.

"On Impulse"

The F on Em7 is a member of B♭7. It is followed by A, anticipating A7.

"On Impulse"

Here are some other delayed resolutions.

"Blessing in Disguise"

"East Broadway Run Down"

"The Everywhere Calypso"

Chord Chart

Root	Major	Minor	Augmented	Diminished	Sixth	Minor Sixth	Seventh	Minor Seventh	Major Seventh	Sus 4
C	C	Cm	C+	C°	C6	Cm6	C7	Cm7	C Ma7	Csus4
Db (C#)	Db	Dbm	Db+	Db°	Db6	Dbm6	Db7	Dbm7	DbMa7	Dbsus4
D	D	Dm	D+	D°	D6	Dm6	D7	Dm7	Dma7	Dsus4
Eb (D#)	Eb	Ebm	Eb+	Eb°	Eb6	Ebm6	Eb7	Ebm7	EbMa7	Ebsus4
E	E	Em	E+	E°	E6	Em6	E7	Em7	E Ma7	Esus4
F	F	Fm	F+	F°	F6	Fm6	F7	Fm7	F Ma7	Fsus4
Gb (F#)	F#	F#m	F#+	F#°	F#6	F#m6	F#7	F#m7	F#Ma7	F#sus4
G	G	Gm	G+	G°	G6	Gm6	G7	Gm7	G Ma7	Gsus4
Ab (G#)	Ab	Abm	Ab+	Ab°	Ab6	Abm6	Ab7	Abm7	AbMa7	Absus4
A	A	Am	A+	A°	A6	Am6	A7	Am7	A Ma7	Asus4
Bb (A#)	Bb	Bbm	Bb+	Bb°	Bb6	Bbm6	Bb7	Bbm7	BbMa7	Bbsus4
B	B	Bm	B+	B°	B6	Bm6	B7	Bm7	B Ma7	Bsus4

God Bless the Child (annotated)

Billy Holiday
and A. Herzog

Sonny Rollins recorded Billy Holiday's "God Bless the Child" with guitarist Jim Hall in 1962 on his first record after rejoining the music scene (*The Bridge*, RCA Victor). This unusual arrangement alternates *a tempo* with out-of-tempo sections. The accompaniment on bass and guitar is carefully arranged and I have tried to transcribe the substitute changes as accurately as possible.

One of Rollins's talents is taking timeworn standards and revitalizing them. In fact, some of his most beautiful recordings are old tunes that other jazz musicians wouldn't touch. He accomplishes this in a number of ways. One of the things that makes this recording unique, for instance, is the instrumentation: guitar, bass, and drums. Jim Hall's playing is particularly beautiful on this cut, and it would be worthwhile to listen once just to his solos. (Catch that wonderful *tremolo* he uses at the end.)

Another special quality of Rollins's ballad playing is his tone. Notice that he rarely plays the notes directly on pitch, but rather slides lazily on and off them. His lack of sharp attacks gives the pieces a hip, laid-back feeling which can make an otherwise corny tune sound like sophisticated jazz.

1. Ⓑ and Ⓒ are repetitions of Ⓐ with rhythmic regrouping, added notes, and a different accompaniment. Guitar enters at Ⓑ.

2. This passage contains many highly dissonant notes. The first note, G♯, clashes with the G of the GMa7/A. The B♮ that follows clashes with the B♭ of the G♭ Ma7/B♭ with which it is played. In essence, Rollins sticks to the notes of B major with which the first two chords conflict. This satisfies the expectation of B major while the guitar and bass play an elaborate chordal substitution.

$\boxed{3}$ $\textcircled{D}$ is Rollins's improvisation on the bridge of "God Bless the Child."

$\boxed{4}$ Diminished seventh run.

$\boxed{5}$ Sequence.

6 B major scale run.

7 Harmony: Rollins jumps up a major seventh from the third of E♭ minor to the ninth. This note is then, briefly, the thirteenth of A♭7 before it descends stepwise to E♮, the flat thirteenth. Excellent voice-leading. Rhythm: repetition of one note.

8. These are all multiphonics, most likely played by overblowing the notes an octave plus a fifth below each note. (See *Improvising Jazz Sax* by Charley Gerard, Consolidated Music Publishers.) The G♯ is the diminished fifth of DMa9. The diminished fifth is frequently added to a major seventh or major ninth at the end of a jazz or pop arrangement.

9. Here Rollins lets the upper octave sound occasionally.

Discography

These are the recordings of the solos I have transcribed in this book. Most of the albums are still in print, or the selections have become available on other albums.

Saxophone Colossus
Prestige PR7326
"You Don't Know What Love Is"

Reevaluation: The Impulse Years
Impulse ABC AS92362
"Alfie's Theme" "On Impulse," "East Broadway Run Down,"
"Blessing in Disguise"

Next Album
Milestone MSP9042
"The Everywhere Calypso," "Playin' in the Yard," "Keep Hold of Yourself"

The Bridge
RCA Victor AFLI0859
"God Bless the Child"